FROM SCARCITY TO ABUNDANCE

The role of positive thinking, self belief and resilience in achieving financial goal

Albert Rogar

Copyright©2024 Albert Rogar

All Rights Reserved.

TABLE OF CONTENT

INTRODUCTION

CHAPTER ONE

THE POWER OF MINDSET

CHAPTER TWO

FINANCIAL HABITS OF HIGH ACHIEVERS

CHAPTER THREE

THE INFLUENCE OF EDUCATION ON WEALTH

CHAPTER FOUR

ENTREPRENEURIAL MINDSET AND WEALTH CREATION

CHAPTER FIVE

GENERATIONAL WEALTH AND SUCCESSION PLANNING:

CHAPTER SIX

IMPACT OF EMOTIONAL INTELLIGENCE ON FINANCIAL SUCCESS

CHAPTER SEVEN

THE PSYCHOLOGY OF RISK-TAKING AND INVESTMENT

CHAPTER EIGHT

PHILANTHROPY AND WEALTH

CHAPTER NINE

CULTURAL AND SOCIETAL INFLUENCES ON WEALTH MINDSET.

CHAPTER TEN

MATERIAL AND NON-MATERIAL WEALTH

CHAPTER ELEVEN

CONCLUSION

INTRODUCTION

Unlocking Financial Abundance

In the pursuit of financial success and prosperity, one often encounters the concept of a "mindset shift." This transformational change in perspective, particularly concerning wealth, has become a focal point in personal development and financial planning. At its core, the mindset shift for wealth transcends mere monetary accumulation; it embodies a holistic approach to abundance, encompassing not only financial riches but also fulfillment, purpose, and freedom.

To embark on this transformative journey, it's crucial to understand the essence of a mindset shift for wealth. It entails a departure from scarcity thinking, which fixates on limitations, fears, and lack, towards embracing abundance mentality. Rather than viewing wealth as a finite resource attainable by only a select few, individuals adopting this mindset recognize the boundless opportunities and possibilities available to them.

Central to this shift is the recognition that wealth encompasses more than just material possessions or monetary wealth. While financial abundance is undoubtedly a significant aspect, true wealth extends to encompass various facets of life, including health, relationships, personal growth, and contributions to society. This holistic perspective fosters a sense of wholeness and fulfillment, transcending the narrow confines of monetary gain.

Moreover, a mindset shift for wealth entails redefining one's relationship with money. Instead of viewing money as a source of stress or anxiety, individuals with an abundance mindset perceive it as a tool for empowerment and liberation. They understand the importance of financial literacy, smart investment strategies, and conscious spending habits in building and preserving wealth over the long term.

Crucially, embracing a mindset shift for wealth requires cultivating a mindset of abundance rather than scarcity. This involves practicing gratitude, focusing on opportunities rather than obstacles, and adopting a growth-oriented mentality.

By shifting their mindset, individuals can tap into their innate potential, unleash creativity, and manifest their desired financial reality.

Furthermore, this mindset shift involves challenging societal narratives and cultural conditioning surrounding wealth. Instead of subscribing to limiting beliefs or comparing oneself to others, individuals embrace their unique path to prosperity, recognizing that success looks different for everyone. This liberation from societal expectations enables individuals to pursue their passions authentically and create their version of wealth and success.

Embracing a mindset shift for wealth is not merely about accumulating riches; it's about cultivating a mindset of abundance, fulfillment, and purpose. By transcending scarcity thinking, redefining their relationship with money, and challenging societal norms, individuals can unlock their full potential and create a life of true abundance. Through conscious awareness and intentional action, anyone can embark on this transformative journey towards financial liberation and prosperity.

CHAPTER ONE

The Power of Mindset

Shifting from Scarcity to Abundance for Wealth Creation

In the pursuit of wealth creation, the role of mindset cannot be overstated. The way individuals perceive opportunities, approach challenges, and envision their financial future plays a crucial role in determining their success. One profound shift that can significantly impact wealth creation is transitioning from a scarcity mentality to an abundance mentality

Understanding Scarcity and Abundance Mentalities:

Scarcity Mentality:
Scarcity mentality is rooted in the belief that resources, opportunities, and success are limited. Individuals with a scarcity mindset often view life as a zero-sum game, where one person's gain must come at the expense of another's loss. This mindset can lead to fear, anxiety,

and a reluctance to take risks, hindering the pursuit of wealth.

Abundance Mentality:
On the other hand, an abundance mentality is characterized by the belief that opportunities are limitless, and there is enough for everyone to succeed. Those with an abundance mindset approach challenges as opportunities for growth and collaboration. This mindset fosters a positive outlook, resilience, and a willingness to take calculated risks, creating a conducive environment for wealth creation.

Impact on Decision-Making:

Risk-Taking and Innovation:
Shifting from scarcity to abundance opens the door to a more proactive approach to risk-taking and innovation. Individuals with an abundance mindset are more likely to embrace calculated risks, recognizing that setbacks are temporary and part of the learning process. This willingness to step outside of comfort zones often leads to groundbreaking ideas and ventures.

Investment Strategies:
Abundance thinkers tend to adopt a long-term perspective on investments. Instead of focusing on

short-term gains or fearing losses, they view investments as vehicles for growth and wealth accumulation over time. This patient approach allows for a diversified and strategic investment portfolio.

Impact on Relationships and Collaboration:

Collaborative Opportunities

The abundance mentality encourages collaboration rather than competition. Individuals who believe in abundance seek out mutually beneficial partnerships and alliances. This collaborative spirit can lead to the creation of innovative businesses, joint ventures, and networks that contribute to wealth creation on a broader scale.

Networking and Mentorship

Abundance thinkers are more likely to seek and provide mentorship. They understand that sharing knowledge and opportunities does not diminish their own chances of success. Engaging in supportive networks and mentorship programs enhances personal and professional development, facilitating wealth creation through shared experiences and insights.

Psychological Well-being and Wealth:

Reduced Stress and Anxiety:
Shifting from a scarcity mindset to an abundance mindset can significantly reduce stress and anxiety associated with financial concerns. The belief in abundance promotes a sense of control over one's financial destiny, leading to a healthier mental state and an increased capacity for strategic decision-making.

Increased Resilience:
Abundance thinkers are more resilient in the face of setbacks. They view challenges as opportunities for growth rather than insurmountable obstacles. This resilience is a crucial factor in navigating the unpredictable nature of financial endeavors and bouncing back from temporary setbacks.

The examination of the shift from a scarcity mentality to an abundance mentality reveals a profound impact on wealth creation. By fostering a positive outlook, encouraging innovation, promoting collaboration, and enhancing psychological well-being, individuals who embrace an abundance mindset position themselves for greater success in their financial pursuits. As the saying goes, "abundance breeds abundance," and this shift in mindset opens doors to opportunities that can lead to sustained and meaningful wealth creation.

The role of positive thinking, self-belief, and resilience in achieving financial success.

Achieving financial success is a journey that extends beyond practical strategies and numerical equations. At its core, it is deeply intertwined with the power of the mind. The triad of positive thinking, self-belief, and resilience forms the cornerstone of a mindset that paves the way for prosperity.

Positive Thinking: The Foundation of Wealth Building

- ❖ **Shaping Reality with Positive Thoughts:** Positive thinking is not merely about wearing a rose-tinted lens; it's about consciously shaping one's reality through optimistic perspectives. When individuals maintain a positive outlook, they are more likely to perceive opportunities in challenges, fostering a proactive approach to wealth creation.

- ❖ **Law of Attraction in Finance:** The law of attraction posits that like attracts like. Positive thinking, according to this principle, can attract positive outcomes. In the financial realm, individuals who radiate positivity often find themselves drawing opportunities, collaborators, and circumstances that align with their optimistic mindset.

- **Mitigating Stress and Fostering Clarity:** Financial endeavors can be riddled with uncertainties and stressors. Positive thinking acts as a buffer, mitigating stress and promoting mental clarity. When faced with financial decisions, those with a positive mindset are better equipped to make sound choices, unclouded by fear or negativity.

Self-Belief: The Catalyst for Financial Confidence

- **Cultivating a Strong Financial Identity:** Self-belief is the foundation upon which financial success is built. Those who believe in their ability to make informed decisions, create wealth, and navigate challenges are more likely to take calculated risks and pursue ambitious goals.

- **Overcoming Imposter Syndrome:** Imposter syndrome, the feeling of inadequacy despite evident success, can hinder financial progress. Self-belief acts as a shield against this phenomenon, empowering individuals to acknowledge their accomplishments and envision themselves as capable contributors to the financial arena.

- ❖ **Empowering Decision-Making:** A strong sense of self-belief empowers individuals to make decisions aligned with their financial goals. This confidence allows for bold moves, such as entrepreneurial ventures or strategic investments, that may be pivotal in the journey towards financial success.

Resilience: The Steadfast Pillar of Financial Triumph

- ❖ **Bouncing Back from Setbacks:** Financial success is rarely a linear path; setbacks and failures are inherent. Resilience, the ability to bounce back from adversity, is crucial in turning challenges into stepping stones. Resilient individuals view setbacks as temporary hurdles rather than insurmountable roadblocks.

- ❖ **Adapting to Changing Circumstances:** The financial landscape is dynamic, with constant fluctuations and unexpected turns. Resilience enables individuals to adapt to changing circumstances, learning from experiences and evolving strategies as needed. This adaptability is vital for long-term financial success.

- ❖ **Maintaining Focus on Long-Term Goals:** Resilience fosters a long-term perspective. Instead of being derailed by short-term failures or market fluctuations, resilient individuals remain focused on their ultimate financial objectives. This steadfast commitment is often a defining factor in enduring success.

In the intricate dance of financial success, positive thinking, self-belief, and resilience are the choreographers guiding every step. Cultivating these mental attributes is not a luxury but a necessity. They transform challenges into opportunities, setbacks into lessons, and aspirations into tangible achievements. As individuals harness the power of this triad, they embark on a journey that transcends monetary gains, leading to a wealth of fulfillment, confidence, and enduring success.

CHAPTER TWO
Financial Habits of High Achievers

The common financial habits and practices of successful individuals.

Behind every story of financial success lies a tapestry of habits and practices that propel individuals toward their goals. These habits, carefully woven into daily routines, play a pivotal role in the journey to financial prosperity.

Strategic Budgeting and Financial Planning:

Successful individuals are meticulous planners. They understand the value of a well-structured budget that allocates funds to various aspects of their lives, from necessities to savings and investments. This strategic approach provides a clear roadmap for financial decisions and ensures that every dollar has a purpose.

Disciplined Savings and Investment Strategies:

Savings are not an afterthought for successful individuals; they are a deliberate and disciplined practice. Whether through automated transfers to savings accounts or regular contributions to investment portfolios, successful individuals prioritize building a financial cushion and creating opportunities for wealth growth over time.

Continuous Learning and Financial Literacy:

Financial success is often rooted in knowledge. Successful individuals commit to ongoing learning about personal finance, investment strategies, and economic trends. They stay informed about market changes, tax implications, and financial instruments, empowering themselves to make informed decisions that align with their goals.

Debt Management and Smart Borrowing:

Successful individuals understand the impact of debt on their financial well-being. They approach borrowing strategically, using debt as a tool for wealth-building rather than as a burden. Managing and reducing debt, especially high-interest debt, is a consistent practice among those who have achieved financial success.

Diversification and Risk Management:

Diversification is a key principle embraced by successful individuals in their investment portfolios. They spread risk across different asset classes, minimizing exposure to any single economic event. This approach, coupled with a clear understanding of risk tolerance, contributes to stable and resilient financial portfolios.

Goal Setting and Long-Term Vision:

Successful individuals are goal-oriented. They set specific, measurable, achievable, relevant, and time-bound (SMART) financial goals. Whether it's saving for a home, funding education, or achieving retirement milestones, a long-term vision guides their financial decisions and instills purpose in their wealth-building endeavors.

Entrepreneurial Spirit and Multiple Income Streams:

Many successful individuals embody an entrepreneurial spirit. They explore and create multiple income streams, whether through side businesses, investments, or real estate ventures. This diversified approach not only enhances financial stability but also opens doors to exponential wealth creation.

Emphasis on Tax Efficiency:
Successful individuals leverage tax-efficient strategies to maximize their wealth. This includes taking advantage of tax-advantaged investment accounts, understanding tax implications before making financial decisions, and engaging with financial professionals to optimize tax efficiency within legal frameworks.

Regular Financial Check-Ins and Adjustments:
Financial success is not a static state; it requires adaptability. Successful individuals conduct regular financial check-ins, assessing their progress, adjusting strategies, and recalibrating goals as needed. This dynamic approach ensures that their financial plans evolve with changing circumstances.

Generosity and Philanthropy:
A striking commonality among successful individuals is a commitment to giving back. Whether through charitable donations, mentorship, or community involvement, they recognize the significance of sharing their success with

others, creating a positive impact beyond their personal wealth.

Investigating the financial habits of successful individuals reveals a tapestry of purposeful actions and disciplined practices. From strategic budgeting to continuous learning and a commitment to giving back, these habits form the foundation of enduring financial success. As individuals adopt and adapt these practices into their own lives, they too can weave a path toward prosperity, navigating the complexities of personal finance with intentionality and resilience.

Budgeting, saving, and investment strategies that contribute to long-term wealth accumulation.

Long-term wealth accumulation is not an overnight endeavor but a strategic and disciplined journey. The pillars of this financial success lie in effective budgeting, consistent saving practices, and well-thought-out investment strategies.

Strategic Budgeting:
- Understanding Income and Expenses:

Successful wealth builders start with a clear understanding of their income and expenses. A comprehensive budget outlines sources of income and categorizes expenditures, providing a roadmap for financial decisions.

> ➤ Prioritizing Needs and Wants:

Budgeting involves making conscious choices about spending. Distinguishing between needs and wants allows individuals to allocate resources to essential areas while curbing unnecessary expenses.

> ➤ Setting Realistic Goals:

A budget is a tool for goal setting. Successful wealth accumulators set realistic financial goals within the framework of their budget, providing a clear vision and motivation for disciplined financial behavior.

Consistent Saving Practices:
> ➤ Emergency Fund Formation:

The foundation of long-term wealth accumulation is often an emergency fund. This financial safety net, built through consistent saving, provides a buffer against unexpected expenses and prevents individuals from dipping into investments during financial crises.

- Automated Savings:

Successful wealth builders often automate their savings. Setting up automatic transfers to savings accounts ensures a consistent flow of funds without relying on willpower alone.

- Incremental Increases:

As income grows, so should savings. Incremental increases in the percentage of income allocated to savings ensure that individuals are consistently building their financial reserves, regardless of fluctuations in income.

Strategic Investment Approaches:

- Diversification:

Long-term wealth accumulation benefits from a diversified investment portfolio. Spreading investments across different asset classes, such as stocks, bonds, and real estate, helps mitigate risk and enhances the potential for stable returns.

- Retirement Planning:

Investing in retirement accounts, such as 401(k)s or IRAs, is a crucial aspect of long-term wealth accumulation.

Taking advantage of employer-sponsored plans and contributing regularly ensures a nest egg for the future.

➢ Continuous Learning and Adaptation:

Markets evolve, and successful investors are lifelong learners. Staying informed about market trends, economic shifts, and emerging investment opportunities allows for informed decision-making and adaptation to changing financial landscapes.

Minimizing Debt and Leveraging Assets:

➢ Responsible Debt Management:

Successful wealth builders understand the impact of debt on long-term financial goals. They manage debt responsibly, focusing on minimizing high-interest debt and strategically leveraging low-interest debt for wealth-building purposes.

➢ Leveraging Assets for Growth:

Real estate, business ownership, and other tangible assets can contribute significantly to long-term wealth. Successful individuals strategically leverage these assets to generate passive income and foster wealth growth.

Regular Review and Adjustment:

➢ Periodic Financial Assessments:

Wealth accumulation is an ongoing process. Regular reviews of budgets, savings plans, and investment portfolios allow individuals to assess progress, make necessary adjustments, and realign strategies with evolving financial goals.

➢ Professional Guidance:

Seeking advice from financial professionals is a prudent step in long-term wealth accumulation. Financial advisors can provide personalized guidance, offer insights into market trends, and assist in optimizing investment strategies.

The journey toward long-term wealth accumulation is a dynamic and intentional process. Effective budgeting, consistent saving practices, and strategic investment approaches form the pillars of financial success. By weaving these principles into their financial habits, individuals not only build a foundation for enduring prosperity but also empower themselves to navigate the complexities of the financial landscape with resilience and purpose.

CHAPTER THREE

The Influence of Education on Wealth

Exploring the correlation between education, continuous learning, and financial success.

In the intricate dance of financial success, education emerges as a formidable partner, shaping not only careers but also the pathways to prosperity. The correlation between education, continuous learning, and financial success is a dynamic synergy that transcends the traditional boundaries of achievement.

Building a Foundation

- Formal Education and Career Opportunities:

Formal education lays the groundwork for career opportunities. A well-rounded education provides individuals with the skills and knowledge necessary to embark on fulfilling and financially rewarding career paths.

- Specialized Knowledge and Marketability:

Specialized education enhances marketability. Whether through a degree, certification, or skill acquisition, individuals with specific expertise often find themselves in high demand, leading to better job prospects and increased earning potential.

Continuous Learning as a Career Catalyst:

Adaptability in a Changing Landscape

Continuous learning is a cornerstone of adaptability. In today's rapidly evolving job market, individuals who embrace lifelong learning demonstrate the ability to adapt to new technologies, industries, and market demands, positioning themselves for sustained career growth.

Professional Development and Skill Enhancement:

Continuous learning fosters professional development. Attending workshops, pursuing additional certifications, and staying abreast of industry trends enhance skill sets, making individuals more valuable assets to employers and clients.

Entrepreneurial Endeavors:

Informed Decision-Making:

Education equips aspiring entrepreneurs with the knowledge required to make informed decisions. Whether it's understanding market dynamics, financial management, or strategic planning, educated entrepreneurs are better positioned to navigate the complexities of starting and running a business.

> ➢ Risk Mitigation through Knowledge:

Entrepreneurs often face risks. Education serves as a risk mitigation tool by providing the knowledge necessary to assess, manage, and minimize potential pitfalls, increasing the likelihood of entrepreneurial success.

Financial Literacy and Smart Decision-Making:

> ➢ Understanding Personal Finance:

Education in financial literacy is a powerful tool for personal financial management. Understanding concepts like budgeting, investing, and debt management empowers individuals to make informed and strategic decisions about their money.

> Investment Savvy:

Continuous learning in the realm of finance equips individuals with the skills to navigate the complexities of investment. Informed investors are better positioned to create and manage portfolios, optimizing returns and contributing to long-term financial success.

Networking and Mentorship Opportunities:

> Educational Networks:

Educational institutions often provide fertile ground for networking. Building connections with peers, professors, and industry professionals opens doors to mentorship opportunities, job referrals, and collaborative ventures that can significantly impact career and financial trajectories.

> Learning from Successful Mentors:

Mentorship is a valuable form of continuous learning. Being guided by successful mentors imparts practical wisdom, insights, and strategies that can accelerate career growth and financial success.

Career Advancement and Salary Growth:

> Higher Degrees and Professional Advancement:

Higher education, such as advanced degrees, is correlated with professional advancement. Individuals with advanced degrees often ascend to higher positions, leading to increased earning potential and financial success.

> ➤ Skills that Command Higher Salaries:

Continuous learning in high-demand skills directly impacts salary growth. Individuals who stay updated with the latest technologies and industry trends often command higher salaries due to their expertise and relevance in the job market.

The correlation between education, continuous learning, and financial success is a dynamic and symbiotic relationship that shapes the trajectories of individuals and their financial well-being. Education not only opens doors to initial career opportunities but also lays the foundation for a mindset of continuous learning, adaptability, and informed decision-making. Embracing a lifelong learning journey equips individuals to navigate the complexities of the ever-evolving professional landscape, positioning them for sustained success and financial prosperity.

Analyzing how acquiring and applying knowledge in areas such as personal finance, investment, and entrepreneurship contributes to wealth-building.

In the intricate tapestry of wealth-building, knowledge emerges as a powerful currency. The acquisition and strategic application of knowledge in key areas such as personal finance, investment, and entrepreneurship form the bedrock of financial success.

Empowering Personal Finance Management:

➢ Budgeting and Financial Planning:

Acquiring knowledge in personal finance allows individuals to master the art of budgeting and financial planning. Understanding income, expenses, and the importance of saving creates a solid foundation for effective financial management.

➢ Debt Management and Credit:

Knowledge in personal finance provides insights into effective debt management and credit utilization.

Informed decisions on borrowing, interest rates, and responsible credit use contribute to financial stability and creditworthiness.

➤ Emergency Fund and Financial Security:

Applying knowledge about the importance of an emergency fund establishes a financial safety net. Individuals with this knowledge are better prepared to navigate unexpected expenses without compromising long-term financial goals.

Strategic Investment Decisions:

➤ Understanding Investment Vehicles:

Knowledge in investment vehicles, such as stocks, bonds, and real estate, enables individuals to make informed investment decisions. Understanding the risk and return profiles of different assets is key to building a diversified and resilient investment portfolio.

➤ Risk Management and Portfolio Diversification:

Acquiring knowledge in risk management strategies allows for the creation of a well-balanced portfolio. Diversification, informed by a deep understanding of various asset classes, helps mitigate risk and optimize returns over the long term.

➢ Long-Term Investing Mindset:

Knowledgeable investors adopt a long-term mindset. They understand the power of compounding and patiently weather market fluctuations, allowing investments to grow steadily over time.

Entrepreneurial Excellence:
➢ Business Planning and Strategy:

Knowledge in entrepreneurship encompasses skills in business planning and strategy. Acquiring this knowledge enables entrepreneurs to create robust business plans, set clear objectives, and develop strategies for sustainable growth.

➢ Market Research and Innovation:

Entrepreneurs armed with knowledge in market research can identify opportunities and gaps in the market. Applying innovative solutions and staying ahead of industry trends contribute to the success and longevity of entrepreneurial ventures.

➢ Financial Management and Scalability:

Financial acumen is crucial for entrepreneurs. Understanding financial statements, cash flow management, and strategic financial decisions contribute to the scalability and profitability of businesses.

Continuous Learning and Adaptability:

➢ Staying Informed in Evolving Landscapes:

The pursuit of knowledge doesn't end; it evolves. Continuous learning ensures individuals stay informed about changes in personal finance, investment trends, and entrepreneurial best practices, fostering adaptability in dynamic environments.

➢ Technological Proficiency

In today's digital age, technological proficiency is a valuable form of knowledge. Embracing new technologies and incorporating them into financial management and business operations enhances efficiency and competitiveness.

➢ Learning from Mistakes and Iteration:

Knowledgeable individuals understand the value of learning from mistakes. This iterative learning process, combined with the ability to adapt strategies based on experience, contributes to resilience and long-term success.

Acquiring and applying knowledge in personal finance, investment, and entrepreneurship is the cornerstone of wealth-building. Informed decision-making empowers individuals to navigate the complexities of financial landscapes, make strategic investments, and embark on entrepreneurial ventures with confidence. As knowledge becomes capital, it transforms aspirations into actionable strategies, paving the way for sustained financial success and the creation of lasting wealth.

CHAPTER FOUR

Entrepreneurial Mindset and Wealth Creation

The entrepreneurial journey is not merely a pursuit of profits; it is a mindset, a way of thinking that transcends challenges and transforms them into opportunities

Embracing Risk as an Opportunity:

➢ Risk-Taking and Calculated Ventures:

The entrepreneurial mindset thrives on calculated risk-taking. Entrepreneurs understand that every venture involves a degree of uncertainty, yet they approach risks with a strategic mindset, evaluating potential rewards and embracing challenges as opportunities for growth.

➢ Fear as a Motivator, Not a Hindrance:

Instead of being paralyzed by fear, entrepreneurs leverage it as a motivator. The entrepreneurial mindset encourages individuals to confront fears, learn from failures, and use setbacks as stepping stones toward innovative solutions.

Visionary Thinking and Opportunity Recognition:

> ➤ Seeing Beyond the Obvious:

Entrepreneurs possess a visionary mindset that enables them to see opportunities where others see challenges. They look beyond the obvious, identify gaps in the market, and envision solutions that have the potential to create significant value.

> ➤ Adapting to Changing Landscapes:

The entrepreneurial mindset is adaptable. Entrepreneurs recognize that markets are dynamic, and the ability to adapt and pivot is crucial. This adaptability ensures that they can spot emerging trends and capitalize on evolving opportunities.

Innovative Problem-Solving:

> ➤ Turning Challenges into Solutions:

Entrepreneurs approach problems as opportunities to innovate. The mindset is geared toward finding creative solutions to challenges, whether it's streamlining processes, improving products, or addressing unmet needs in the market.

> Iterative Learning and Continuous Improvement:

Failure is not a roadblock; it's a feedback loop. The entrepreneurial mindset values iterative learning, where each setback becomes a lesson, leading to continuous improvement and refinement of strategies.

Resilience and Grit:

> Bouncing Back from Setbacks:

The entrepreneurial mindset is characterized by resilience. Entrepreneurs view failures not as the end but as a part of the journey. They bounce back from setbacks, learning and adapting with an unwavering determination to succeed.

> Grit in the Face of Adversity:

Grit is a defining trait of the entrepreneurial mindset. Entrepreneurs persevere in the face of challenges, often working tirelessly toward their goals. This resilience contributes to the ability to weather storms and emerge stronger.

Customer-Centric Focus:

> Understanding Customer Needs:

Entrepreneurs prioritize understanding the needs of their customers. The entrepreneurial mindset is customer-centric, focusing on creating products or services that provide real value and address the pain points of their target audience.

> ➤ Building Relationships and Loyalty:

Customer loyalty is not just a result; it's a strategic objective. Entrepreneurs cultivate relationships with their customers, seeking feedback, and adapting their offerings based on the evolving needs and preferences of their audience.

Passion and Commitment:

> ➤ Fueling Action with Passion:

The entrepreneurial mindset is fueled by passion. Entrepreneurs are driven by a genuine love for what they do, which propels them to put in the hard work and dedication required for long-term success.

> ➤ Commitment to the Vision:

Commitment is unwavering in the entrepreneurial mindset. Entrepreneurs remain dedicated to their vision, even in the face of challenges. This steadfast commitment is essential for navigating the ups and downs of the entrepreneurial journey.

The entrepreneurial mindset is a force that propels individuals to think beyond conventional boundaries, take calculated risks, and innovate in the pursuit of wealth creation. By embracing risk, envisioning opportunities, and persistently problem-solving, entrepreneurs transform challenges into stepping stones toward sustainable and innovative wealth. As a mindset that values resilience, customer-centricity, and unwavering commitment, it becomes the driving force behind not just financial success, but the creation of

lasting value in the entrepreneurial landscape.

Highlighting the risk-taking, adaptability, and resilience required for entrepreneurial success.

The entrepreneurial journey is an exhilarating expedition into the unknown, and its success is often sculpted by the courage to take risks, the ability to adapt to changing landscapes, and the unwavering resilience to face challenges head-on

Risk-Taking: Navigating Uncharted Waters

Calculated Ventures:
Entrepreneurs are not reckless gamblers; they are calculated risk-takers. They assess potential risks, weigh them against potential rewards, and embark on ventures with a strategic understanding of the uncertainties involved.

Innovation through Risk:
Risk is the crucible of innovation. Entrepreneurs understand that groundbreaking ideas often reside on the precipice of uncertainty. By taking risks, they push the boundaries of what is possible and pave the way for transformative solutions.

Embracing Failure as a Stepping Stone:
Failure is not a deterrent but a catalyst for growth. Entrepreneurs view failure as an inherent part of the journey, extracting valuable lessons that contribute to future success. Each setback becomes a stepping stone toward eventual triumph.

Adaptability: Navigating the Shifting Tides

Dynamic Market Landscapes:
The business landscape is dynamic, subject to constant evolution. Entrepreneurs with adaptability ingrained in their mindset are quick to respond to changes in market trends, consumer behavior, and technological advancements.

Pivoting with Purpose:
Adaptability is not about veering off course; it's about strategic pivoting. Successful entrepreneurs pivot with purpose, aligning their strategies with the evolving needs of their target audience and the demands of the market.

Learning from Feedback:
Adaptability involves a willingness to listen and learn. Entrepreneurs actively seek feedback, whether from customers, mentors, or market trends, and use this information to iterate on their products, services, and overall business strategies.

Resilience: Weathering the Entrepreneurial Storms

Bouncing Back from Setbacks:
Resilience is the armor that shields entrepreneurs from the inevitable setbacks. Whether facing financial challenges, market downturns, or unexpected hurdles, resilient entrepreneurs bounce back, learning from each experience and growing stronger.

Enduring Passion and Vision:
Resilience is fueled by an enduring passion for the vision. Entrepreneurs driven by a deep-seated belief in their mission weather storms with tenacity. This passion acts as a compass, guiding them through challenges and keeping the vision alive.

Building Mental Toughness:
Entrepreneurship is a mental marathon. Resilient entrepreneurs build mental toughness, cultivating the ability to stay focused, optimistic, and solution-oriented even in the face of adversity. This mental fortitude is a key asset in the entrepreneurial toolkit.

In the realm of entrepreneurship, risk-taking, adaptability, and resilience are not just traits; they are the dynamic forces that propel visionaries toward success. By embracing calculated risks, adapting to changing landscapes, and remaining resilient in the face of challenges, entrepreneurs navigate the complexities of their journey with courage and determination. As these pillars interweave, they create a foundation upon which entrepreneurial triumphs are not just achieved but celebrated as a testament to the indomitable spirit of those who dare to dream and act.

CHAPTER FIVE

Generational Wealth and Succession Planning

The concept of generational wealth and how successful individuals plan for the transfer of wealth to future generations.

Generational wealth is more than the accumulation of financial assets; it's a legacy that transcends time, providing opportunities and security for future generations. Successful individuals understand that the transfer of wealth is a delicate and strategic process that involves not just the distribution of assets but the cultivation of values, knowledge, and a vision for the future.

Defining Generational Wealth:

Beyond Monetary Assets

Generational wealth encompasses not only financial assets but also intellectual, social, and cultural capital. It is a holistic approach to preserving and enhancing the well-being of future generations.

Sustainability and Longevity:

The concept goes beyond immediate gains, focusing on sustainable practices that ensure wealth endures across multiple generations. It involves strategic planning to maintain and grow assets over the long term.

Components of Generational Wealth:

Financial Capital

This includes investments, real estate, businesses, and other monetary assets. Successful individuals build and manage their financial capital with an eye on longevity and stability.

Educational and Intellectual Capital:

Generational wealth involves the transfer of knowledge and intellectual capital. This may include educational opportunities, mentorship, and the sharing of experiences to empower the next generation.

Social and Cultural Capital:

Successful individuals often prioritize the transfer of social and cultural capital. This involves instilling family values, traditions, and a sense of identity that enriches the family legacy.

Strategic Succession Planning:

Open Communication:
Transparent communication is vital in succession planning. Successful individuals engage their family members in open discussions about wealth, values, and the responsibilities tied to the family legacy.

Professional Guidance:
Many successful individuals seek the assistance of financial advisors, estate planners, and legal professionals to ensure a comprehensive and legally sound succession plan. This involves structuring assets in a way that minimizes taxes and facilitates a smooth transfer.

Education and Mentorship:
Beyond financial planning, successful individuals invest in the education and mentorship of the next generation. This prepares heirs to responsibly manage wealth and make informed decisions about the family's assets.

Balancing Preservation and Growth:

Preserving Core Values
Successful individuals recognize the importance of preserving the core values that contributed to their

success. They instill these values in the younger generation, ensuring a continuity of principles that guided the family's achievements.

Adapting to Changing Times

The ability to adapt the family's wealth management strategies to changing economic, social, and technological landscapes is crucial. Flexibility ensures that the family legacy remains relevant and resilient across generations.

Philanthropy and Social Impact:

Charitable Initiatives:

Many successful families integrate philanthropy into their generational wealth plans. Establishing charitable foundations or participating in community initiatives allows them to create a positive social impact that extends beyond financial contributions.

Teaching the Importance of Giving Back:

Generational wealth involves instilling a sense of responsibility for giving back to society. Successful individuals teach the next generation the importance of using their resources to contribute to the greater good.

Generational wealth is a dynamic concept that extends beyond material possessions. It involves a thoughtful and strategic approach to ensuring the continuity of financial stability, values, and opportunities for future generations. Successful individuals recognize the importance of planning, communication, and adaptability in building a legacy that transcends time, leaving an indelible mark on the family's history and the broader community.

The strategies for effective succession planning and wealth preservation.

The transfer of wealth from one generation to the next requires more than financial transactions; it demands a strategic and comprehensive succession plan. Successful individuals understand the significance of proactive planning to ensure the seamless transition of assets and values

Establishing Clear Objectives:

Defining Family Goals

The foundation of effective succession planning is built upon clearly defined family goals. Successful individuals engage family members in discussions to identify shared values, financial objectives, and the desired legacy they wish to leave behind.

Setting Individual Roles and Responsibilities:

Assigning specific roles and responsibilities to family members within the wealth management structure helps ensure clarity and accountability. Each individual's strengths and interests should be considered when delineating responsibilities.

Open and Transparent Communication:

Family Meetings and Discussions:

Regular family meetings provide a platform for open communication about financial matters, expectations, and the overall vision for the future. Transparency helps mitigate potential conflicts and ensures that everyone is on the same page.

Educating the Next Generation:

Successful succession planning includes educating the next generation about financial management, the family's values, and the responsibilities tied to wealth. Workshops, mentorship programs, and ongoing communication foster a culture of understanding and collaboration.

Engaging Professional Advisors:

Financial and Legal Experts:
Enlisting the expertise of financial advisors, estate planners, and legal professionals is crucial. These professionals help structure the succession plan, navigate tax implications, and ensure that all legal requirements are met.

Business Succession Planning:
For individuals with family businesses, a specific focus on business succession planning is essential. This involves identifying and preparing potential leaders within the family or external management, ensuring a smooth transition of business operations.

Diversifying and Protecting Assets:

Asset Diversification:
Successful wealth preservation involves diversifying assets across different classes, reducing risk exposure. A well-balanced portfolio protects against market fluctuations and economic uncertainties.

Risk Management Strategies:

Implementing risk management strategies, such as insurance policies, helps safeguard the family's financial well-being. Adequate protection against unforeseen events, including health crises or market downturns, is integral to wealth preservation.

Implementing Trusts and Legal Structures:

Trusts for Wealth Transfer:

Trusts are powerful tools for wealth transfer. Establishing trusts allows for the efficient distribution of assets, minimizes probate issues, and provides a structured approach to passing wealth to beneficiaries.

Legal Frameworks for Governance:

Implementing legal frameworks, such as family constitutions or governance structures, helps define decision-making processes and dispute resolution mechanisms. These structures provide a framework for future generations to follow.

Continual Monitoring and Adjustment:

Regular Reviews
The dynamics of both family and financial landscapes evolve. Regular reviews of the succession plan ensure that it remains aligned with changing circumstances, legal requirements, and the family's evolving goals.

Adapting to Economic Changes:
Economic conditions can impact the performance of investments. Successful succession planning involves monitoring economic trends and adjusting investment strategies to capitalize on opportunities and mitigate risks.

Introducing Philanthropy and Social Responsibility:

Establishing Family Philanthropic Initiatives:
Introducing philanthropy as part of the family's legacy promotes social responsibility. Establishing family charitable foundations or contributing to community initiatives becomes a shared goal that extends beyond financial wealth.

Teaching the Value of Giving Back:

Wealth preservation is not just about financial assets; it's about preserving the family's values. Incorporating a commitment to giving back to society instills a sense of purpose and responsibility in future generations.

Effective succession planning and wealth preservation require a holistic and forward-thinking approach. Successful individuals recognize that the key to securing the future lies in clear communication, engaging professional expertise, and adapting strategies to changing circumstances. By combining financial acumen with a commitment to family values, they create a legacy that endures, providing opportunities and stability for generations to come.

CHAPTER SIX

Impact of Emotional Intelligence on Financial Success

The role of emotional intelligence in making sound financial decisions.

Money is not just a transactional tool; it carries with it a web of emotions, values, and aspirations. The ability to navigate the intricate landscape of personal finance requires more than just analytical skills; it demands emotional intelligence

Self-Awareness and Financial Goals:

Understanding Personal Values:
Emotional intelligence begins with self-awareness. Individuals with a high level of emotional intelligence understand their core values, which play a pivotal role in shaping financial goals. Aligning spending and saving habits with these values creates a foundation for sound financial decisions.

Clarifying Financial Objectives:

Emotionally intelligent individuals take the time to clarify their financial objectives. Whether it's saving for a home, planning for retirement, or paying off debt, a clear understanding of these goals guides decision-making and fosters financial discipline.

Emotional Regulation in Budgeting:

Managing Impulse Spending:

Budgeting requires emotional regulation, particularly when faced with impulsive spending urges. Emotionally intelligent individuals can recognize and manage these impulses, ensuring that financial decisions align with long-term goals rather than momentary desires.

Stress Management and Financial Anxiety:

Financial decisions are often accompanied by stress and anxiety. Emotional intelligence enables individuals to manage these emotions effectively, preventing them from clouding judgment and leading to impulsive or fear-driven financial choices.

Empathy in Financial Relationships:

Understanding Partner's Perspectives:
For those in financial partnerships, empathy plays a crucial role. Emotionally intelligent individuals understand and respect their partner's perspectives on money, fostering open communication and joint decision-making.

Negotiating Financial Compromises:
Financial decisions may involve compromises. Emotionally intelligent individuals can navigate these negotiations with empathy, finding solutions that satisfy both parties and maintain financial harmony.

Social Skills in Investment and Networking:

Building Financial Networks:
Successful financial endeavors often involve networking and collaboration. Emotionally intelligent individuals excel in building and maintaining relationships, creating opportunities for shared financial knowledge, investment partnerships, and mutual support.

Negotiating and Collaborating in Investments:

Investment decisions may require negotiation and collaboration. Emotionally intelligent investors can navigate these interactions with finesse, whether it's partnering with others on a venture or negotiating terms for mutual benefit.

Motivation and Long-Term Financial Discipline:

Sustaining Financial Motivation:
Financial journeys are marathons, not sprints. Emotionally intelligent individuals can sustain motivation over the long term, drawing on their intrinsic drive and passion for their financial goals.

Resilience in Financial Setbacks:
Financial setbacks are inevitable, and emotional intelligence equips individuals with the resilience to bounce back from challenges. Rather than succumbing to despair, emotionally intelligent individuals learn from setbacks and adjust their financial strategies.

Making Decisions in Changing Economic Environments:

Adaptability to Economic Shifts:
Economic changes can trigger emotional responses, from fear during a downturn to overconfidence in a boom. Emotionally intelligent individuals adapt to changing economic environments, making decisions grounded in realistic assessments rather than emotional reactions.

Cautious Optimism in Windfalls:
Windfalls, whether through bonuses or unexpected gains, can evoke strong emotions. Emotionally intelligent individuals approach windfalls with cautious optimism, balancing the excitement of newfound resources with a strategic and disciplined financial plan.

The emotionally intelligent wallet is not just about numbers; it's about understanding and managing the intricate interplay between emotions and finances. By cultivating self-awareness, regulating emotions, and navigating financial relationships with empathy, emotionally intelligent individuals make sound financial decisions that align with their values and long-term goals. In the ever-changing landscape of personal finance, emotional intelligence emerges as the compass that guides individuals toward financial well-being and resilience.

How emotional resilience and interpersonal skills contribute to successful wealth management.

In the realm of wealth management, success is not solely determined by market trends and financial acumen. Emotional resilience and interpersonal skills stand as formidable pillars, influencing how individuals navigate the complexities of wealth.

Emotional Resilience in Financial Setbacks:

Navigating Market Volatility:
Financial markets are inherently volatile, subject to fluctuations that can trigger emotional responses. Emotional resilience empowers individuals to weather the storms of market turbulence without succumbing to fear or making impulsive decisions.

Learning from Losses:

Resilience involves not just bouncing back from financial setbacks but learning from them. Emotionally resilient individuals use setbacks as opportunities for growth, adapting their strategies and gaining valuable insights to inform future wealth management decisions.

Stress Management in High-Stakes Decision-Making:

Executive Decision-Making Under Pressure:

Wealth management often involves high-stakes decision-making. Emotional resilience enables individuals to manage stress effectively, making clear-headed decisions even in the midst of pressure.

Preventing Emotional Biases:

Emotional resilience acts as a safeguard against cognitive biases that can cloud judgment. Individuals who can manage stress are less prone to emotional decision-making biases, ensuring a more rational and strategic approach to wealth management.

Building and Nurturing Client Relationships:

Empathy in Client Interactions:
Successful wealth management goes beyond numbers; it involves understanding and empathizing with clients' unique situations and goals. Interpersonal skills allow wealth managers to build strong client relationships founded on trust and understanding.

Clear Communication and Transparency:
Interpersonal skills facilitate clear communication. Wealth managers with strong interpersonal skills can explain complex financial concepts in a way that clients can understand, fostering transparency and trust in the wealth management relationship.

Collaborating with Financial Professionals:

Team Collaboration in Wealth Planning:
Wealth management often involves collaboration with a team of financial professionals, including advisors, lawyers, and accountants. Strong interpersonal skills enhance the ability to work cohesively within a team, ensuring a comprehensive approach to wealth planning.

Negotiation and Networking Skills:

Negotiating favorable terms, whether in investments or partnerships, requires adept interpersonal skills. Wealth managers who excel in negotiation can secure advantageous deals and build a network that enriches their clients' wealth management strategies.

Succession Planning and Family Dynamics:

Facilitating Family Discussions:

Succession planning involves delicate family discussions. Emotional resilience enables wealth managers to navigate the emotional dynamics of family relationships, ensuring that financial decisions align with both the family's goals and individual aspirations.

Conflict Resolution:

Interpersonal skills play a pivotal role in resolving conflicts within families. Wealth managers who are adept at conflict resolution can guide families through challenging discussions, fostering unity and collaboration in matters of wealth management.

Adapting to Changing Client Needs:

Understanding Evolving Priorities:
Client needs and priorities evolve over time. Emotional resilience allows wealth managers to adapt to these changes, responding with flexibility and empathy as clients navigate life transitions, such as retirement or the passing of a family member.

Anticipating Emotional Responses:
Anticipating and understanding clients' emotional responses to financial decisions is crucial. Wealth managers with strong emotional intelligence can tailor their approach, providing support and guidance that aligns with clients' emotional well-being.In the intricate tapestry of wealth management, emotional resilience and interpersonal skills emerge as vital threads that weave together financial success and human dynamics. Beyond charts and spreadsheets, the ability to navigate emotional terrain, build strong relationships, and adapt to the evolving needs of clients and families defines the art of successful wealth management. By embracing these elements, wealth managers not only safeguard financial assets but also nurture enduring partnerships that transcend market trends, contributing to a legacy of financial prosperity and emotional well-being.

CHAPTER SEVEN

The Psychology of Risk-Taking and Investment

The psychological factors influencing risk tolerance in wealth creation.

The world of wealth creation is not only shaped by economic principles and market dynamics but also by the intricate workings of the human mind. Risk tolerance, a critical factor in investment decisions, is a psychological phenomenon influenced by a myriad of factors

Perception of Risk:

Subjectivity of Risk Perception:

Risk, in the financial context, is not an absolute value but a subjective perception. Individuals interpret risk differently based on their experiences, beliefs, and the information available to them. Past experiences, whether positive or negative, can significantly shape how individuals perceive risk in future investment opportunities.

Cognitive Biases:

Cognitive biases, such as loss aversion and recency bias, play a pivotal role in shaping risk perception. Loss aversion makes individuals more averse to potential losses than gains of equal magnitude, while recency bias causes people to give more weight to recent events when evaluating risks.

Personality Traits:

Risk-Seeking vs. Risk-Averse:

Personality traits play a crucial role in determining risk tolerance. Some individuals have a natural inclination toward risk-seeking behaviors, thriving on the excitement of uncertainty. Others are inherently risk-averse, preferring stability and predictability. Personality assessments, such as the Big Five personality traits, can provide insights into an individual's natural risk predisposition.

Overconfidence:

Overconfidence can lead to an overestimation of one's ability to predict and control outcomes. Overconfident individuals may exhibit higher risk tolerance, believing they can beat the market or outperform the average investor. This bias can influence decision-making, potentially leading to riskier investment choices.

Financial Knowledge and Experience:

Educational Background:
The level of financial knowledge and education influences how individuals approach risk. Those with a solid understanding of financial principles may feel more confident in their ability to assess and manage risks, impacting their risk tolerance.

Experience in the Markets:
Past experience in the financial markets shapes risk tolerance. Individuals who have weathered market fluctuations and experienced both gains and losses may develop a more realistic and resilient attitude toward risk, while those with limited experience may be more cautious or prone to emotional reactions.

Temporal Perspectives:

Time Horizon:
The time horizon for wealth creation significantly influences risk tolerance. Long-term investors may tolerate more short-term volatility, recognizing that market fluctuations are part of the journey. In contrast,

individuals with a shorter time horizon may lean toward conservative, lower-risk investments to protect their capital.

Present vs. Future Orientation:

An individual's temporal perspective, whether oriented more toward the present or the future, can impact risk tolerance. Those focused on immediate rewards may be more inclined to take higher risks, while individuals with a future-oriented mindset may prioritize long-term stability over short-term gains.

Social and Cultural Influences:

Social Norms and Peer Influence:

Social norms and peer influence contribute to risk tolerance. Individuals may be swayed by the behavior of their social circles or influenced by prevailing cultural attitudes toward risk. The fear of deviating from societal norms can impact risk-taking behavior.

Cultural Attitudes Toward Risk:

Cultural backgrounds shape attitudes toward risk. Cultures that value entrepreneurship and risk-taking may foster individuals with higher risk tolerance, while cultures emphasizing stability and security may lead to a more conservative approach to wealth creation.

Emotional Regulation:

Emotional Intelligence:
Emotional intelligence, including the ability to manage emotions effectively, influences risk tolerance. Emotionally intelligent individuals can navigate the emotional roller coaster of investing, making decisions based on rational analysis rather than succumbing to fear or greed.

Fear and Greed Dynamics:
The emotions of fear and greed, inherent in financial markets, can significantly impact risk tolerance. Fear may lead to risk aversion, causing individuals to withdraw from the markets during downturns. Conversely, greed may drive individuals to take excessive risks in pursuit of high returns.

Wealth creation is not a sterile process governed solely by economic principles; it is a deeply human endeavor shaped by the intricacies of the mind. The psychological factors influencing risk tolerance weave a complex tapestry that defines how individuals approach investments, navigate uncertainties, and ultimately carve their path toward financial success. By understanding and acknowledging these psychological nuances, investors and wealth managers can make more informed decisions, crafting strategies that align with individual risk profiles and fostering a resilient and prosperous journey toward wealth creation.

Discussing the mindset and decision-making processes of successful investors.

Behind every successful investor lies a unique combination of mindset, discipline, and decision-making prowess. The world of investing is not merely a numbers game; it's a complex interplay of psychological traits and strategic approaches.

Long-Term Vision and Patience:

Strategic Horizon:
Successful investors possess a long-term vision that extends beyond short-term market fluctuations. They understand that wealth creation is a gradual process, requiring patience and a commitment to the strategic goals they've set.

Endurance Through Volatility:
In the face of market volatility, successful investors remain steadfast. They view market downturns not as

crises but as opportunities to accumulate assets at lower prices, confident in the eventual recovery of well-chosen investments.

Disciplined Approach to Risk:

Calculated Risk-Taking:
Successful investors are not reckless gamblers. Their approach to risk is calculated and strategic. They assess potential risks, conduct thorough research, and make informed decisions that align with their risk tolerance and long-term objectives.

Risk Management Strategies:
A disciplined investor employs risk management strategies. Diversification, setting stop-loss orders, and having an exit strategy are integral components of their approach, minimizing the impact of adverse market movements.

Continuous Learning and Adaptability:

Curiosity and Continuous Education:
Successful investors have an insatiable curiosity about the financial markets. They engage in continuous learning, staying abreast of industry trends, economic indicators, and emerging opportunities.

Adapting to Market Changes:

The financial landscape is dynamic, and successful investors are adept at adapting to changes. They pivot their strategies when necessary, recognizing that staying ahead requires flexibility and the ability to capitalize on evolving market conditions.

Emotional Intelligence and Rational Decision-Making:

Emotional Resilience:

Successful investors exhibit emotional resilience. They can navigate the psychological highs and lows of investing without succumbing to fear or greed. Emotional intelligence allows them to make rational decisions based on analysis rather than emotional reactions.

Decisiveness in the Face of Uncertainty:

When faced with uncertainty, successful investors do not succumb to indecision. They make decisive choices based on available information, understanding that waiting for absolute certainty may lead to missed opportunities.

Focus on Fundamentals:

Deep Fundamental Analysis:
Successful investors prioritize fundamental analysis. They delve deep into the financial health of companies, studying balance sheets, cash flows, and growth prospects. Their decisions are grounded in a thorough understanding of the underlying assets.

Value Investing Principles:
Many successful investors adhere to value investing principles. They seek out undervalued assets, focusing on intrinsic value rather than short-term market sentiment. This disciplined approach aligns with the long-term wealth-building vision.

Contrarian Thinking:

Going Against the Crowd:
Contrarian thinking is a hallmark of successful investors. They are not swayed by market hype or popular sentiments. Instead, they often go against the crowd, recognizing that opportunities may arise where others see challenges.

Buying Opportunities in Market Pessimism:
During periods of market pessimism, successful investors see potential buying opportunities. They view undervalued assets as a chance to build positions that will reap rewards when market sentiment eventually turns.

Focus on Quality and Management:

Quality Over Quantity:
Successful investors prioritize quality over quantity in their portfolios. They prefer a concentrated portfolio of high-quality assets rather than a scattered approach. This emphasis on quality aligns with a commitment to long-term value creation.

Assessment of Leadership and Governance:
They assess not only a company's financials but also its leadership and governance. A strong management team and effective governance contribute to the overall quality of an investment.

The success of investors is not solely determined by financial acumen; it is deeply rooted in mindset and decision-making processes. Successful investors embrace a long-term vision, exercise discipline in risk management, and exhibit continuous learning. Their emotional intelligence and rational decision-making set them apart, allowing them to navigate market complexities with resilience and decisiveness. By adhering to fundamental analysis, contrarian thinking, and a focus on quality, successful investors carve a path to financial triumph that transcends market fluctuations and stands the test of time.

CHAPTER EIGHT

Philanthropy and Wealth

Examining the relationship between wealth and philanthropy.

The relationship between wealth and philanthropy is a dynamic interplay that extends beyond financial transactions. Wealth, when wielded with a philanthropic spirit, becomes a powerful force for positive change in communities and societies.

Wealth as a Catalyst for Philanthropy:

Enabling Generosity:
Wealth provides the means to be generous. Philanthropy, rooted in a desire to make a positive difference, is empowered by the financial resources that wealth affords. Individuals and families with significant wealth have the capacity to contribute to causes they are passionate about on a substantial scale.

Fulfilling Social Responsibility:
Wealth comes with a sense of social responsibility. Many affluent individuals recognize the privileges that accompany financial success and feel compelled to give

back to society. Philanthropy becomes a channel through which they actively address societal challenges and contribute to the well-being of others.

Philanthropy as a Source of Fulfillment:

Beyond Financial Rewards:
While wealth often brings financial rewards, philanthropy provides a different form of enrichment. The act of giving, whether through charitable donations, community development, or social initiatives, offers a sense of fulfillment and purpose that goes beyond monetary gains.

Creating a Lasting Legacy:
Philanthropy allows individuals to create a lasting legacy. By directing wealth toward causes aligned with their values, philanthropists leave an indelible mark on the world. Foundations, endowments, and charitable initiatives become enduring symbols of their commitment to positive change.

Strategic Philanthropy:

Impactful Resource Allocation:
Wealthy individuals can engage in strategic philanthropy, directing resources toward initiatives that

can create meaningful and sustainable impact. This involves thoughtful consideration of where and how resources can be most effectively utilized to address systemic issues and drive positive change.

Leveraging Influence for Social Good:
Wealthy philanthropists often leverage their influence to advocate for social change. Beyond monetary contributions, they use their positions to influence policies, raise awareness, and catalyze collective action toward addressing pressing societal issues.

The Philanthropic Ecosystem:

Collaboration with Nonprofits and NGOs:
Wealth and philanthropy thrive within a collaborative ecosystem. Wealthy individuals often partner with nonprofits, non-governmental organizations (NGOs), and other stakeholders to amplify the impact of their contributions. This collaborative approach enhances the effectiveness of philanthropic efforts.

Supporting Innovation and Research:
Philanthropy can fuel innovation and research. Wealthy donors can contribute to advancements in science, technology, and various fields by funding research

initiatives and supporting projects that have the potential to bring about transformative change.

Impact on Global Challenges:

Addressing Global Issues:
Wealthy individuals have the capacity to address global challenges. Philanthropy can play a pivotal role in tackling issues such as poverty, healthcare disparities, environmental sustainability, and education. Through targeted giving, wealth can be channeled toward solutions that transcend geographical boundaries.

Humanitarian Aid and Crisis Response:
Wealthy philanthropists often play a crucial role in humanitarian aid and crisis response. Their contributions can provide rapid relief in the aftermath of natural disasters, pandemics, and other emergencies, showcasing the agility and responsiveness of philanthropy.

The relationship between wealth and philanthropy is a harmonious one, where financial success becomes a catalyst for positive change. Wealth, when channeled through philanthropy, has the potential to uplift communities, drive social progress, and address pressing global challenges. The impact of this symbiotic relationship extends far beyond monetary transactions, leaving a legacy of compassion, empowerment, and a shared commitment to building a better, more equitable world. As wealth and philanthropy continue to intersect, the potential for transformative change grows, showcasing the inherent capacity of financial resources to be a force for good.

How successful individuals use their resources to make a positive impact on society.

Success is not merely about personal accomplishments; it is an opportunity to effect positive change on a broader scale. Successful individuals, armed with resources and influence, often become agents of societal transformation.

Strategic Philanthropy:

Targeted Giving:
Successful individuals engage in strategic philanthropy, directing their resources toward causes aligned with their values. This involves careful consideration of societal issues, needs, and opportunities, ensuring that

their contributions have a meaningful and lasting impact.

Establishing Foundations:
Many high achievers establish foundations as vehicles for their philanthropic endeavors. Foundations provide a structured approach to giving, allowing for sustained impact through initiatives, grants, and programs that address specific challenges.

Social Entrepreneurship:

Investing in Solutions:
Successful individuals often embrace social entrepreneurship, investing in ventures that aim to address social and environmental challenges. They leverage their business acumen and resources to create sustainable solutions, fostering innovation for the greater good.

Supporting Social Enterprises:
High achievers recognize the potential of social enterprises to drive positive change. They support and invest in businesses that prioritize social impact alongside financial sustainability, contributing to a shift toward more socially responsible and ethical business practices.

Advocacy and Influence:

Using Platforms for Advocacy:
Success often comes with increased visibility and influence. Successful individuals leverage their platforms to advocate for social causes. They use their voices to raise awareness, champion policy changes, and address systemic issues that require broader societal attention.

Lobbying for Change:
High achievers may engage in lobbying efforts to influence policymakers and institutions. By using their influence strategically, they seek to shape legislation and policies that align with their philanthropic goals, contributing to systemic change.

Investing in Education:
Scholarships and Educational Initiatives:

Investing in education is a common avenue for making a positive impact. Successful individuals establish scholarship programs and educational initiatives to provide opportunities for learning and skill development, particularly for those with limited access.

Supporting Educational Institutions:
Many high achievers contribute to the enhancement of educational institutions. Endowments, infrastructure development, and funding for research centers are ways in which resources are directed toward creating a robust and accessible educational environment.

Community Development:

Local and Global Community Initiatives:
Successful individuals often invest in community development initiatives. This can involve supporting local projects that enhance infrastructure, healthcare, and overall quality of life. Additionally, some extend their impact globally by addressing issues such as poverty, clean water access, and healthcare in underserved regions.

Entrepreneurial Ecosystem Support:
High achievers who have experienced entrepreneurial success may support the growth of the entrepreneurial ecosystem in their communities. This could include funding startup incubators, mentoring emerging entrepreneurs, or investing in local businesses to stimulate economic development.

Environmental Stewardship:

Sustainable Practices in Business:
Successful individuals who are business leaders often integrate sustainable practices into their organizations. This includes reducing carbon footprints, implementing eco-friendly technologies, and adopting environmentally responsible business strategies.

Conservation and Restoration Initiatives:
Resources are directed toward environmental conservation and restoration projects. This can involve supporting initiatives that protect biodiversity, preserve natural habitats, and address climate change through innovative solutions.

The use of resources by successful individuals to make a positive impact on society represents a commitment to a broader vision of success—one that transcends personal achievements to create a meaningful and lasting legacy. Whether through strategic philanthropy, social entrepreneurship, advocacy, or community development, high achievers recognize the transformative power of their resources to contribute to a more equitable, sustainable, and compassionate world. As these individuals continue to leverage their success for societal benefit, the ripple effects of their contributions extend far beyond individual accomplishments, shaping a collective future of positive change.

CHAPTER NINE

Cultural and Societal Influences on Wealth Mindset.

Attitudes towards wealth and success are not universal; they are deeply rooted in the cultural and societal contexts in which individuals find themselves.

Cultural Values and Priorities:

Collectivism vs. Individualism:

Cultures vary in their emphasis on collectivism or individualism. In collectivist societies, success may be measured in terms of contributions to the community or family harmony. Individualistic cultures may prioritize personal achievements and financial success as indicators of a fulfilling life.

Spiritual and Material Balance:

Some cultures emphasize a balance between spiritual and material pursuits. Success is not solely measured by wealth but also by spiritual growth, wisdom, and the well-being of the community. Others may place a higher premium on material wealth as a sign of prosperity and success.

Cultural Narratives and Perceptions:

Rags-to-Riches vs. Contentment Narratives:
Cultural narratives play a crucial role in shaping attitudes towards success. Cultures that embrace rags-to-riches stories may view financial success as a testament to hard work and determination. In contrast, cultures emphasizing contentment narratives may value a simple and fulfilled life over material accumulation.

Cultural Symbols of Success:
Different cultures have distinct symbols of success. While some may equate success with academic achievements, others may prioritize familial accomplishments, such as marriage or parenthood. Cultural symbols contribute to the diverse spectrum of what is deemed valuable and successful.

Societal Norms and Expectations:

Educational and Professional Pursuits:
Societal norms often influence educational and career aspirations. In some cultures, academic excellence is a cornerstone of success, while others may place more emphasis on vocational or entrepreneurial pursuits.

These norms shape the paths individuals choose in their quest for success.

Work-Life Balance and Well-being:
Societal expectations around work-life balance vary. Cultures that value well-being may prioritize leisure, family time, and health over relentless career pursuits. In contrast, societies emphasizing industriousness may associate long working hours with dedication and success.

Social Class and Mobility:

Attitudes Towards Social Mobility:
Cultural and societal factors influence attitudes towards social mobility. In some societies, there is a belief in upward mobility and the ability to transcend one's social class through hard work. Conversely, others may exhibit skepticism or barriers to social mobility, impacting attitudes towards wealth accumulation.

Inherited vs. Earned Wealth:
Societal attitudes towards inherited wealth also vary. Some cultures celebrate family legacies and generational wealth, considering it a sign of stability and success. Conversely, societies may view self-made wealth as a more commendable and equitable form of success.

Cultural Perspectives on Wealth Redistribution:

Views on Wealth Redistribution:
Societal attitudes towards wealth redistribution reflect cultural values. Some cultures endorse policies and practices that promote wealth redistribution, aiming for a more equitable society. Others may resist such measures, viewing them as a threat to individual success and entrepreneurial spirit.

Philanthropy and Social Responsibility:
Cultural perspectives on philanthropy and social responsibility differ. Some cultures prioritize collective welfare and view philanthropy as an integral part of success. Others may be more individualistic, with a focus on personal achievements rather than societal contributions.

Impact of Historical and Economic Contexts:

Historical Trajectories and Cultural Memory:
Historical events shape cultural attitudes towards wealth and success. Cultures that have experienced economic hardships may have a more cautious or conservative

approach to financial matters. Historical traumas or periods of prosperity contribute to the collective cultural memory that influences contemporary attitudes.

Globalization and Cultural Influences:

Globalization has led to the blending of cultural influences. Societies exposed to global media and economic systems may experience shifts in attitudes towards success, with an increasing emphasis on cosmopolitan values that transcend traditional cultural boundaries.

Attitudes towards wealth and success form a complex mosaic, intricately woven by the threads of culture and society. Understanding the diverse influences that shape these attitudes is essential for appreciating the rich tapestry of human perspectives. As cultures evolve and societies undergo transformations, so too will the nuanced ways in which individuals perceive and pursue success, reflecting the ever-changing interplay between cultural values and societal dynamics.

The impact of cultural values on financial goals and decision-making.

Culture serves as a silent architect shaping our perceptions, beliefs, and behaviors, including those related to financial goals and decision-making.

Cultural Definitions of Success:

Collectivist vs. Individualistic Cultures:
In collectivist cultures, success may be intertwined with family achievements, community recognition, and harmonious relationships. Contrastingly, individualistic cultures often associate success with personal accomplishments, financial independence, and the pursuit of individual goals.

Spiritual vs. Material Success:
Some cultures emphasize the spiritual and non-material aspects of success, valuing qualities like wisdom, generosity, and community service. Others place a higher premium on material wealth as a tangible indicator of success, equating financial achievements with prosperity and well-being.

Savings and Investment Priorities:

Long-Term vs. Short-Term Orientation:
Cultural attitudes towards time orientation influence financial decision-making. Cultures with a long-term orientation may prioritize savings and investments for future security, while those with a short-term orientation may lean towards immediate consumption and gratification.

Community vs. Individual Goals:
Cultures valuing community goals may prioritize collective savings for events like weddings or festivals over individual investment portfolios. In contrast, cultures emphasizing individual pursuits may encourage personal financial goals and wealth accumulation.

Educational and Career Choices:

Cultural Perceptions of Prestige:
The cultural perception of prestigious professions greatly influences educational and career choices. Some cultures prioritize fields like medicine, law, or engineering for their perceived stability and prestige, while others may place high value on entrepreneurial ventures and artistic pursuits.

Family Expectations:

Cultural expectations within families can play a significant role. In some cultures, children may be expected to pursue specific careers to maintain family traditions or contribute to the family's social standing. This can impact financial decision-making regarding educational investments and career paths.

Attitudes Toward Debt:

Cultural Stigma or Acceptance of Debt:

The cultural stigma or acceptance of debt varies widely. In some cultures, debt is frowned upon, and financial decisions revolve around avoiding indebtedness. In contrast, cultures with a more accepting attitude towards debt may view it as a tool for achieving financial goals, such as homeownership or education.

Generational Perspectives:

Cultural values passed down through generations influence attitudes towards debt. Some cultures prioritize financial independence and discourage reliance on credit, while others may view borrowing as a pragmatic means to achieve specific life milestones.

Wealth Redistribution and Philanthropy:

Collectivism and Social Responsibility:
Cultures emphasizing collectivism often prioritize wealth redistribution and social responsibility. Financial goals may include contributing to community projects, supporting extended family members, or participating in philanthropy as a way of giving back to society.

Individual Prosperity and Personal Philanthropy:

In cultures valuing individual prosperity, financial goals may revolve around personal wealth accumulation. However, individuals from such cultures may still engage in personal philanthropy, aligning with values of personal responsibility and the desire to make a positive impact.

Risk-Taking and Financial Conservatism:

Risk Aversion vs. Risk Tolerance:
Cultural attitudes towards risk greatly influence financial decision-making. Cultures with a higher risk tolerance may encourage entrepreneurial ventures and investment in potentially high-yield assets. Conversely,

risk-averse cultures may prioritize financial stability and conservative investment strategies.

Cultural Responses to Economic Downturns:

Cultural values impact responses to economic downturns. Some cultures may encourage resilience and perseverance, viewing challenges as temporary setbacks. Others may emphasize caution and conservative financial strategies during uncertain times.

Cultural values act as invisible hands guiding financial aspirations and decision-making. Whether determining definitions of success, influencing savings priorities, shaping educational and career choices, or impacting attitudes towards debt and risk, culture weaves a profound narrative in the financial lives of individuals. Understanding this interplay is crucial for financial institutions, policymakers, and individuals alike, as it allows for a more nuanced and culturally sensitive approach to financial planning and decision-making in our diverse global landscape.

CHAPTER TEN

Material and Non-material Wealth

The concept of holistic wealth, encompassing not only financial prosperity but also well-being, fulfillment, and life satisfaction.

In a world often fixated on financial prosperity, the concept of holistic wealth emerges as a beacon, casting a broader light on the multifaceted nature of a truly fulfilling life. Holistic wealth transcends the narrow confines of monetary riches, encompassing dimensions of well-being, personal fulfillment, and life satisfaction.

Financial Prosperity as One Component:

Beyond Material Wealth

Holistic wealth acknowledges the importance of financial prosperity but underscores that it is just one facet of a well-rounded life. While financial stability provides security and opportunities, true wealth extends beyond material possessions to encompass a spectrum of human experiences.

Financial Freedom for Pursuing Dreams:
Financial prosperity is seen as a means to an end, granting individuals the freedom to pursue their passions, invest in personal growth, and contribute to the well-being of themselves and others.

Physical and Mental Well-Being:

Health as a Fundamental Asset:
Holistic wealth places a premium on health as an indispensable component. Physical well-being lays the foundation for an active and fulfilling life, while mental health ensures emotional resilience and cognitive flourishing.

Balancing Work and Rest:
Achieving holistic wealth involves maintaining a delicate balance between professional endeavors and personal well-being. Prioritizing sufficient rest, exercise, and mental rejuvenation contributes to a sustainable and thriving lifestyle.

Personal Growth and Development:

Continuous Learning and Skill Enhancement:
Holistic wealth embraces a mindset of continuous learning and skill enhancement. Personal growth and

development are considered integral to a fulfilling life, encouraging individuals to explore new interests, acquire knowledge, and evolve both personally and professionally.

Cultivating Emotional Intelligence:

Emotional intelligence is recognized as a cornerstone of holistic wealth. The ability to navigate and understand one's emotions, as well as empathize with others, contributes to richer relationships, effective communication, and overall life satisfaction.

Meaningful Relationships:

Quality Connections Over Quantity:

Holistic wealth places emphasis on the quality of relationships rather than sheer quantity. Nurturing meaningful connections with family, friends, and the broader community contributes significantly to a sense of fulfillment and belonging.

Cultivating Empathy and Compassion:

The ability to empathize and show compassion towards others is regarded as an essential aspect of holistic wealth. Building a supportive and interconnected community contributes to a sense of purpose and well-being.

Purpose and Contribution:

Finding Meaning in Contributions:
Holistic wealth encourages individuals to find purpose and meaning in contributing to something larger than themselves. Whether through philanthropy, community service, or meaningful work, a sense of purpose adds profound depth to life satisfaction.

Aligning Personal Values with Contributions:

Contributing to causes aligned with personal values enhances the sense of purpose. Holistic wealth involves aligning financial resources and efforts with causes that resonate deeply, fostering a sense of fulfillment and impact.

Work-Life Integration:

Balancing Professional and Personal Aspects:
Holistic wealth challenges the traditional notion of work-life balance and proposes work-life integration. It advocates for aligning professional pursuits with personal values, creating a seamless and harmonious integration of one's professional and personal life.

Flexible and Fulfilling Careers:
Pursuing careers that align with personal passions and values is central to holistic wealth. This approach fosters a sense of fulfillment, satisfaction, and purpose in professional endeavors.

Holistic wealth stands as an invitation to redefine success, urging individuals to embark on a journey that goes beyond the accumulation of financial assets. It encompasses the richness of well-being, personal fulfillment, and life satisfaction. By embracing holistic wealth, individuals can cultivate a life that is not only financially prosperous but also deeply meaningful, balanced, and fulfilling. It is an affirmation that true wealth extends beyond bank balances, encompassing the richness of human experiences that contribute to a life well-lived.

The importance of balance in pursuing both material and non-material aspects of wealth.

In the pursuit of a fulfilled and meaningful life, the concept of balance emerges as a guiding principle, reminding us that true wealth encompasses both material and non-material dimensions.

Material Wealth as a Foundation:

Financial Security and Opportunities:
Material wealth, in the form of financial stability, provides a foundational layer for a secure and comfortable life. It opens doors to opportunities, affording individuals the means to meet their basic needs, pursue education, and invest in personal and professional growth.

Freedom to Choose:
Acquiring material wealth grants individuals the freedom to make choices that align with their aspirations. Whether it's choosing a fulfilling career, investing in experiences, or contributing to causes, material wealth serves as a tool for empowerment and self-determination.

Non-Material Wealth for Enrichment:

Emotional Well-Being and Fulfillment:
Non-material wealth, encompassing aspects like emotional well-being and personal fulfillment, adds a profound layer of richness to life. Nurturing positive

emotions, experiencing joy, and finding purpose contribute immeasurably to a life well-lived.

Quality Relationships and Connections:
The non-material dimension of wealth extends to the quality of relationships and connections. Building meaningful bonds with family, friends, and the community enhances the human experience, providing a sense of belonging, support, and shared joy.

Harmony in Work and Life:

Work as a Source of Fulfillment:
Achieving balance involves viewing work not just as a means to financial ends but as a source of personal fulfillment. Pursuing a career aligned with personal values and passions contributes to a harmonious integration of professional and personal life.

Boundaries and Well-Being:
Striking a balance between work and personal life is crucial for overall well-being. Setting boundaries, prioritizing self-care, and nurturing personal interests outside of work create a sustainable and fulfilling lifestyle.

Philanthropy and Contribution:

Material Resources for Impact:
Material wealth offers the means to contribute meaningfully to societal well-being. Whether through philanthropy, community service, or environmentally conscious choices, individuals can leverage their material resources for positive impact.

Emotional Wealth in Giving:
Non-material wealth is deeply embedded in acts of giving and contribution. The emotional wealth derived from making a positive difference in the lives of others enhances personal fulfillment, emphasizing the interconnectedness of material and non-material dimensions.

Mindful Consumption and Experiences:

Balancing Material Consumption:
Mindful consumption involves striking a balance between acquiring material possessions and recognizing the limits of their impact on happiness. Emphasizing quality over quantity and deriving joy from experiences rather than possessions contribute to a balanced approach.

Investing in Experiences:

Non-material wealth thrives in the realm of experiences. Investing in travel, education, and meaningful activities fosters personal growth, broadens perspectives, and contributes to a life rich in memories and fulfillment.

Financial Planning with Life Goals:

Aligning Financial Goals with Life Aspirations:

A balanced approach to financial planning involves aligning material wealth goals with broader life aspirations. Setting financial objectives that support personal growth, family well-being, and contributions to the community ensures a holistic and purpose-driven wealth strategy.

Flexibility and Adaptability:

Balance requires flexibility and adaptability in financial planning. Acknowledging that life is dynamic, with evolving goals and circumstances, allows for adjustments that align with changing priorities in both material and non-material dimensions.

The pursuit of true wealth is a delicate dance, requiring the mindful navigation of both material and non-material dimensions. By recognizing the symbiotic relationship between financial prosperity and personal fulfillment, individuals can strive for a balanced life that is not only prosperous but also deeply meaningful. It is in the harmonious integration of material and non-material wealth that individuals discover the richness of a life well-balanced and purposefully lived.

CHAPTER ELEVEN
conclusion

The journey towards wealth creation is not solely about accumulating monetary assets; it is a profound inner transformation that transcends material gain. Embracing a mindset shift for wealth creation involves adopting an abundance mentality, redefining our relationship with money, and challenging societal narratives surrounding success. By cultivating gratitude, focusing on opportunities, and embracing our unique path to prosperity, we unlock our full potential to manifest financial abundance. This shift in mindset empowers us to navigate challenges, make informed decisions, and pursue our passions authentically. Ultimately, the journey towards wealth creation is a holistic endeavor that encompasses personal growth, fulfillment, and the realization of our highest aspirations. Through conscious awareness and intentional action, we can embark on this transformative journey and create a life of true abundance and prosperity.

the concept of a mindset shift for wealth creation is a profound journey that transcends mere financial accumulation. It represents a transformative shift in our perception, beliefs, and behaviors towards money and abundance. This shift encompasses a holistic approach to prosperity, emphasizing not only material wealth but also personal fulfillment, purpose, and well-being.

One of the fundamental aspects of this mindset shift is the transition from scarcity thinking to abundance mentality. Rather than dwelling on limitations, fears, and lack, individuals embrace the idea that opportunities are limitless and that abundance is available to all. By cultivating gratitude, focusing on abundance, and acknowledging the abundance that already exists in our lives, we open ourselves up to receiving more wealth and opportunities.

Furthermore, redefining our relationship with money is crucial in the mindset shift for wealth creation. Instead of viewing money as a source of stress or anxiety, we recognize it as a tool for empowerment and liberation. This involves developing financial literacy, adopting smart investment strategies, and practicing conscious spending habits. By understanding the value of money and leveraging it wisely, we can build and preserve wealth over the long term.

Moreover, challenging societal norms and cultural conditioning surrounding wealth is essential in this mindset shift. Rather than conforming to traditional notions of success or comparing ourselves to others, we embrace our unique path to prosperity. This involves letting go of limiting beliefs, embracing our strengths and talents, and pursuing our passions authentically. By following our own definition of success and creating our version of wealth, we can live a more fulfilling and purpose-driven life.

In essence, the mindset shift for wealth creation is about cultivating a mindset of abundance, empowerment, and possibility. It requires conscious awareness, intentional action, and a willingness to challenge the status quo. By embracing this mindset shift, we unlock our full potential, tap into our innate creativity, and manifest our desired financial reality. Ultimately, wealth creation becomes not just a goal but a journey of personal growth, fulfillment, and the realization of our highest aspirations.

www.ingramcontent.com/pod-product-compliance
Lightning Source LLC
Chambersburg PA
CBHW050316230526
45471CB00005B/2212